FREED TO BE GOD'S PEOPLE

Bible Studies from Exodus

ROBIN KIMBROUGH

Copyright © 2005 by Abingdon Press. All rights reserved.

With the exception of those items so noted, no part of this work may be reproduced or transmitted in any form or by any means, electronic or mechanical, including photocopying and recording, or by any information storage or retrieval system, except as may be expressly permitted by the 1976 Copyright Act or in writing from the publisher. Requests for permission should be addressed to Abingdon Press, 201 Eighth Avenue, South, P.O. Box 801, Nashville, TN 37202-0801.

Unless otherwise noted, Scripture quotations are from the *New Revised Standard Version of the Bible*, copyright © 1989, Division of Christian Education of the National Council of the Churches of Christ in the United States of America. Used by permission. All rights reserved.

05 06 07 08 09 10 11 12 13 14—10 9 8 7 6 5 4 3 2 1

MANUFACTURED IN THE UNITED STATES OF AMERICA

Cover Design by Keely Moore

CONTENTS

STUDY 1: Phenomenal Women
(Exodus 1:14-22; 2:10) **1**

STUDY 2: Excuses, Excuses, Excuses
(Exodus 3:7-15) **14**

STUDY 3: Let My People Go
(Exodus 11:4-10; 12:29-32) **25**

STUDY 4: How Do You Get Water
From a Rock?
(Exodus 17:1-7) **39**

STUDY 5: Freedom Has a Price
(Exodus 20:1-20)...................**51**

STUDY 6: Give Me a Break
(Exodus 31:12-17) **64**

STUDY 7: A Stiff-Necked People
(Exodus 32:7-14)................**77**

This Bible study focuses on three key tools for exciting Bible study: comprehension, interpretation, and application.

What's the Text? begins by simply reading the Scripture passage for what it says. Then it invites deeper understanding by having us examine and ask questions about the text.

What's the Context? looks at both the literary issues and the cultural and social situation. The information in this section may address specific terms used in the passage, the character of the particular book of the Bible, what comes before the passage, what comes after it, and the events and cultural expectations of the times. Having this "story behind the story" provides important information for understanding the text and its meaning.

What's Next?, the third section, recognizes that studying the Bible is not focused on information, but on transformation. Here's where we intentionally focus on today by looking at different "Views" that relate to contemporary life.

One reason for doing Bible study this way is to learn *how* to study the Bible. As your group works through text, context, and what's next, you will be learning an important skill for a lifetime of encountering God's Word.

The real joy in engaging this Living Word is its power to change our lives—for the better. You don't have to get "right" answers; you do have to be open and searching—and the Spirit will lead you.

Visit www.ileadyouth.com/3V for
- student-leader helps
- background on the Gospels
- worship suggestions
- contents of the other studies in the 3V series

LEADING THE STUDIES

Adult and Student Leaders
Adults or high school students can lead or co-lead these studies. Interested students can facilitate the whole study or lead a particular discussion or activity for their peers. By using small groups at particular points, all students will gain more experience as both leaders and participants.

Students who have been student-leaders for *Synago* are especially qualified to lead all or portions of these 3V Bible Studies. Go to *www.ileadyouth.com* for student-leader helps and for more information about *Synago* for senior highs.

Activities
As you lead, don't hesitate to try some of the more active ideas (roleplay or drawing, for example). Sometimes the physical and verbal cues of a one-minute roleplay lead to great new insights. Another reason to try the activities is that different people learn in different ways. So expand the opportunities for everyone to learn.

Group Size
All size groups of senior highs can easily use this study method. If your group is small, do most of the sections together, with occasional conversations in pairs or threes. If the group is larger, break into small groups or pairs more often, with times of reporting and talking as a whole group.

Bibles
Everyone should have access to a study book and a Bible. Have a variety of translations of the Bible available. Referring to the different translations is a helpful skill in Bible study. Sometimes subtle nuances in the wording can give more clarity or insight. Sometimes they help raise good questions.

The New Revised Standard Version (NRSV) is printed here so that students can feel good about writing in their books. They can highlight words and phrases they think are important or note questions that the Scripture passage raises for them, which they might not do in a Bible.

FITTING YOUR TIME

This approach to Bible study is very flexible. You may choose to:

- Do all of a particular study or streamline it;
- Do the study in one session or over two or three;
- Do all the questions, or choose some;
- Do some of the studies or all of them.

If you need to spend less time, plan to do What's the Text? and What's the Context? You may wish to deal with fewer of the questions in each section. Be sure to do After Looking at Both the Text and the Context.

If you have more time, add View You (U) in What's Next? If you have still more time, use one or all of the other Views (A, B, C) for some spirited debate.

Suggested Schedule Options

One Session Only
5–10 minutes	What's the Text?
20–25	What's the Context? (Selected Questions)
20–35	What's Next? (Selected Views)
5–10	View You

Two Sessions
10–15 minutes	What's the Text?
20–30	What's the Context? (Selected Questions)
10–15	What's Next (One View)
10–15 minutes	Review of Text and Context
30–40	What's Next? (Remaining Views)
5–10	View You

Three Sessions
1. Do What's the Text? and What's the Context? (Most Questions)
2. Do a review of Text and Context; finish any remaining Context sections and After Looking at Both the Text and the Context.
3. Do a brief review of previous sessions; choose one or more of the Views in What's Next? Close with View You. Consider using the Worship Suggestions from *www.ileadyouth.com/3V*.

PHENOMENAL WOMEN

Exodus 1:14-22; 2:10

When we think of the great figures of the Old Testament, we often think of men: Abraham, Jacob, Joseph, Moses, Joshua, David. On the surface, women seem to be left out of biblical history. But read closer. If you've heard that God made women to be weak and subservient to men, God has a message for you in this Scripture. And you may be surprised to learn how brave, compassionate women—even a woman outside of God's chosen people—play key roles in bringing forth God's plan.

2

¹⁴ And [the Egyptians] made [the Israelites'] lives bitter with hard service in mortar and brick and in every kind of field labor. They were ruthless in all the tasks that they imposed on them.

¹⁵ The king of Egypt said to the Hebrew midwives, one of whom was named Shiphrah and the other Puah, ¹⁶ "When you act as midwives to the Hebrew women, and see them on the birthstool, if it is a boy, kill him; but if it is a girl, she shall live." ¹⁷ But the midwives feared God; they did not do as the king of Egypt commanded them, but but they let the boys live. ¹⁸ So the king of Egypt summoned the midwives and said to them, "Why have you done this, and allowed the boys to live?" ¹⁹ The midwives said to Pharaoh, "Because the Hebrew women are not like the Egyptian women; for they are vigorous and give birth before the midwife comes to them." ²⁰ So God dealt well with the midwives; and the people multiplied and became very strong. ²¹ And because the midwives feared God, [God] gave them families. ²² Then Pharaoh commanded all his people, "Every boy that is born to the Hebrews you shall throw into the Nile, but you shall let every girl live."

. . . .

¹⁰ When the child grew up, [the baby's mother] brought him to Pharaoh's daughter, and she took him as her son. She named him Moses, "because," she said, "I drew him out of the water."

Exodus 1:14-22; 2:10, NRSV

Read the text aloud. Then have participants read silently from as many different versions as possible and report any differences in the wording.

- What questions do you have from reading the text? Make a list.

List on a markerboard or large sheet of paper the women in this Scripture. Work together to write beside each woman's name any words that the group believes describe that character's traits and emotions as the story unfolds.

List your initial responses to what is happening in the text. What would you have done if you were:

❏ Moses' mother? Why would you have done this?
❏ a Hebrew midwife? Why would you have done this?
❏ Pharaoh's daughter? Why would you have done this?

- How does looking at the text through the lens of these different characters affect your view of the Scripture? Why?

4

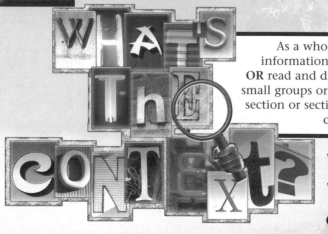

As a whole group, read through this information and discuss the questions; **OR** read and discuss the commentaries in small groups or pairs assigned to a specific section or sections. Then summarize your conversation for the others.

WHO WERE GOD'S PEOPLE?

Humankind originated with the creation of Adam. Through Adam comes Abraham. God made a covenant with Abraham and Sarah, that they would birth many nations and that these nations—including the twelve tribes of Israel—would live with God under the covenant. Genesis tells how these nations descended from Abraham through Isaac then through Jacob (whom God renamed "Israel"). Most of the Old Testament tells the story of Abraham and Sarah's direct descendants. But some Old Testament stories reveal that this covenant extends to non-Israelites. Through these accounts, God reveals that anyone who believed in God was one of God's people and could benefit from God's covenant with Abraham and Sarah. The latter chapters of Genesis tell God's people's struggles to realize God's promise. The final five chapters reveal how famine struck the Israelites and how God uses an evil act against Joseph by his brothers (the sons of Israel) to preserve the nation of Israel in Egypt.

- How do you define God's people, based on your understanding of Scripture? List some characteristics that describe a "person of God."
- Do you think that we are all God's people just because we are all a part of God's creation? Explain.
- How do you think freedom plays a role in a person's being one of God's people?

DISRESPECTING JOSEPH

Exodus 1:8 tells us that "a new king arose over Egypt, who did not know Joseph." Well, duh! Several hundred years have passed between the end of Genesis and the opening of Exodus. Of course the pharaoh of the Exodus would not know Joseph. What's going on here?

Historians suggest one possibility. The pharaohs during and after what we believe to be Joseph's time were not purely Egyptian but Hyksos (HICK-sohs). Like the Israelite tribes, the Hyksos were a Semitic people from beyond Egypt's traditional boundaries; as such, a Hyksos pharaoh may have been sympathetic to Joseph and his fellow Semites. But the Hyksos dynasty ended before the time of Moses, meaning that Hyksos policies ended too.

Many scholars believe that Rameses II, who ruled during much of the thirteenth century B.C., was the pharaoh of the Exodus. He and his father, Seti I, were nationalistic and distrustful of foreigners. In this environment, feeling threatened by the Hebrews' growing population, Pharaoh conspires to enslave the Israelites and limit their numbers.

- Why do you think Pharaoh enslaves the Israelites? How might his motives be political? economic? What role might fear play?
- How are foreigners viewed today as a threat by the people of a country? Give some examples.
- How do you identify with the Israelites as foreign victims of discrimination?
- What would be the point of view of the Egyptians? How do you identify with them?

THEY LOOKED THE OTHER WAY

To prevent the Israelite population from growing, Pharaoh commands two midwives, Shiphrah and Puah, to kill all newborn Hebrew males upon delivery. Why would he choose these women? Why doesn't he just order Egyptian soldiers to kill the baby boys?

First, delivering babies is a midwife's job. (Even in advanced societies like ours, many women who wish to have their babies at home employ midwives, who are trained professionals.) These women would know much better than Egyptian officials where and when the Hebrew babies were born.

Second, if Pharaoh doesn't want it to be widely known that he is having babies killed, choosing midwives for his purpose would make sense, because at various stages throughout the delivery they could make a baby's death appear to be an accident or the result of a common complication.

Finally, Pharaoh likely thinks that he can easily take advantage of these medical professionals because, as women, they are viewed as weak and, in any case, have no authority to disobey his orders. These women, however, choose to look the other way. They fear God (that is they respect God's power) more than they fear the king. Although the Pharaoh is the most powerful man in Egypt—making him among the most powerful in the world—Shiphrah and Puah do not stand by passively. They risk their lives to save the children.

- What do Shiphrah and Puah's actions say about their relationship with God? Are they simply more afraid of God than of Pharaoh? What motivates them?
- When have you disobeyed someone in authority because you knew that it was the right thing to do? What happened?
- How do Pharaoh's prejudices work against him?
- Christians believe in telling the truth. How do you think God viewed the midwives' lying to Pharaoh?
- How does God bless the midwives? Notice that they are named in the Scripture but the king is not. Why do you think that is?

PHARAOH PUTS OUT A HIT ON MOSES

When Pharaoh's plan to use the midwives to murder the male children fails, he orders his Egyptian followers to kill the male newborns. Note that Pharaoh does none of his own dirty work. He enlists others.

- Why do you think Pharaoh orders the deaths of male babies, instead of females? How would the male-dominated culture of the Egyptians and Israelites figure into Pharaoh's decision?

Read **Exodus 2:1-10.** These verses recount the birth of Moses, who, as a male child, was to be thrown in the Nile. Technically, that's what his mother does. She hides him for three months; then she and her daughter Miriam sail him down the river in a water-tight basket. Can you imagine all of the things Moses' mother has to do to keep a three-month-old, crying baby hidden?

- In what way does Moses' mother act in faith?
- How is her act one of resistance?
- Exodus does not even reveal the name of Moses' mother. But what can we guess about her character from the story?

The text says that Moses' mother and sister wait to see what will happen to Moses after they place him in the water. But the Scripture also hints that Miriam might know that Pharaoh's daughter will be coming to the river to bathe at just this time of day.

- How would putting Moses in a basket still be an act of faith even if Miriam knows that Pharaoh's daughter will find him?
- List what you think might have gone through Miriam's mind as she stood lookout and then approached Pharaoh's daughter.

8

ANOTHER WOMAN TO THE RESCUE

Pharaoh's daughter finds Moses, shows compassion for him, and adopts him as her son. The blessing unfolds when Miriam suggests that a Hebrew woman nurse the child and fetches her (and Moses') mother. Moses apparently does not live under the roof of Pharaoh's daughter until he is older.

Yet Pharaoh's daughter is not a passive figure in the drama. Her actions are critical to the fulfillment of God's promise. In adopting Moses, she boldly disobeys her father's orders about killing baby Israelite boys.

- Why do you think Pharaoh's daughter disobeys her father, the king?
- Do you think that Pharaoh's daughter really wants to be a mother, or is she—out of compassion—focused on saving this one child?
- Describe how you think Moses' mother might have felt about raising a child whom she could not acknowledge as her own?

The Egyptians are the bad guys in the Exodus saga. Yet God acts through an Egyptian woman to preserve the covenant that God had made with Abraham.

- What does this story suggest about God's view of (or relationship with) non-Israelites?
- What does this Scripture suggest about how God works through women in societies where women have little or no formal authority?

AFTER READING THE TEXT AND THE CONTEXT …

Deal with some or all of these questions before moving to What's Next?

- What new insights do you have?

- What answers have you gained to questions you raised earlier?

- What do you admire about the Chosen people? Where in their story do you see God's favor? Where in your life do you see God's favor?

- What do you know about your family background? How does this knowledge influence how you feel about yourself?

- What does this text say about jealousy? about hatred? about love? about God?

- What does the text suggest about motherhood and sisterhood?

- How is this story empowering for women?

- How do you balance your faith in God with obedience to your parents or school rules?

- What one learning will you take from this Scripture and apply to your life?

10

Choose one or more of Views A, B, and C to discuss; OR have different small groups talk about one and then summarize the discussion for the other groups. **Be sure to have everyone complete View U.**

VIEW A: WOMEN ARE FROM VENUS, MEN ARE FROM MARS

In Egypt, the Israelite women were enslaved not only by Pharaoh but also by sexism, racism, and poverty. Their world is not as remote to us as we might imagine. Not until 1920 were women allowed to vote in the United States. Women today often bump up against "glass ceilings"—facing unspoken limits on what they are allowed to accomplish professionally, academically, athletically, socially, and politically. They are often stereotyped as the weaker sex, in need of male protectors. In many ways, women of different backgrounds still struggle to find a voice in a society that has traditionally silenced them and treated them as inferiors.

Yet in the ancient stories of Moses' birth, rescue, and upbringing, God stands tradition on its head with a radical truth: Women are necessary for the protection of men. Although Egyptian society is patriarchal (male dominated), women still act with their own minds and strength. They stand up to authority and for God. In a society where men have all of the formal power, God chooses women to be the instruments for preserving the covenant.

- Do you believe that men and women have distinct roles, with one being subservient to the other? How does your understanding of Scripture affect your view?
- Should some activities or responsibilities be performed by only men? by only women Which activities or responsibilities?
- Why might men and women misunderstand one another? What power struggles contribute to this misunderstanding?
- In what ways is our society patriarchal? our church? How is the balance of power changing?

CHILDBEARING CHALLENGES

Raising children who are born into difficult circumstances is often quite challenging. Some parents are able to rear their sons and daughters in these trying situations, but others choose a different route. Moses' mother has to abandon him because Pharaoh has ordered all newborn Hebrew males put to death. Fortunately, through Miriam's maneuvering (and God's hand at work), Moses' mother still participates in raising her son.

Many children are not as fortunate as Moses. In the time of American slavery, some slave mothers abandoned or even murdered their children to spare them the horrors of bondage, which could include brutal rapes and beatings. Other slave children were sold and separated from one or both parents.

These challenges continue today. Antwone Fisher was one of many children who spent years in foster care because his parents could not adequately care for him. Fisher wrote a book (*Finding Fish*—Perennial, 2001), which became a movie (*Antwone Fisher*—Twentieth Century Fox, 2003) about his experiences growing up in an abusive foster care system. Many people look down on mothers who give their children up for adoption. But in most cases, being adopted proves to be the best chance for the child to have a successful life.

- What emotions do you think Moses' mother felt as she prepared to abandon him? How do you think her feelings would compare with emotions of women today who give up their children for adoption or to foster care?
- Aside from giving them up, how do parents abandon their children today?
- Why might adoption sometimes be a better option for some parents and children? What are the other options?
- In what ways are children in foster care at a disadvantage compared with children raised by their parents?

PASSIVE RESISTANCE

The Hebrews of this story are slaves. They lack the power to fight actively against their oppressors. Yet they find creative ways to thwart the will of their Egyptian masters. The midwives disobey and lie to Pharaoh, who apparently accepts their story. Moses' mother disobeys Pharaoh's command to kill her son.

It is little wonder that slaves in America were attracted to the stories of Moses and the Israelites in Egypt. Like the midwives, American slaves also used passive resistance. They deliberately slowed down the pace of work (leading masters to think that they were simply lazy). They sometimes sabotaged farm implements and told their overseers that the tools simply broke.

And sometimes they were helped by latter-day Pharaoh's daughters: free Americans—both white and black—who sheltered runaway slaves, even though they were breaking the law in doing so.

- Why resist passively against a system you cannot hope to replace?
- In recent years, how have people practiced passive resistance against oppressive systems? Name some examples of people and movements of passive resistance that have changed history. Tell some of the stories.
- In what ways do you, as a Christian, feel called to practice passive resistance against oppression or against practices and values in society that run counter to your faith?

CRACKED POTS?

Moses, the mothers of the dead male babies, and the other enslaved Israelites may have thought that God had abandoned them. When really bad things happen to us, we too may feel that God has left us alone and forgotten about us.

The Israelites had been enslaved for almost four hundred years. Their freedom would ultimately come "in God's own good time." Sometimes it's hard to wait for God or to operate on God's time frame.

But we also have the assurance that, when God's people cried out for help, God heard them and responded. (See **Exodus 2:23-25**.) That assurance, as much as anything from God's original covenant with Abraham, is God's promise to us: God hears our prayers, feels our suffering, and comes to help.

Write your reflections on the following question:

- How does God come to you in your bad times? How do you ask God to come to you?

Check www.ileadyouth.com/3V
for worship suggestions.

14

EXCUSES, EXCUSES, EXCUSES

Exodus 3:7-15

We all have anxieties about attempting things that we don't know how to do or have never done before. When God calls us to do one of these uncomfortable tasks, there's bad news and good news. The bad news: God does not excuse us from answering the call. But the good news: When God is with you, you don't need to make excuses.

7 Then the LORD said, "I have observed the misery of my people who are in Egypt; I have heard their cry on account of their taskmasters. Indeed, I know their sufferings, 8 and I have come down to deliver them from the Egyptians, and to bring them up out of that land to a good and broad land, a land flowing with milk and honey, to the country of the Canaanites, the Hittites, the Amorites, the Perizzites, the Hivites, and the Jebusites. 9 The cry of the Israelites has now come to me; I have also seen how the Egyptians oppress them. 10 So come, I will send you to Pharaoh to bring my people, the Israelites, out of Egypt." 11 But Moses said to God, "Who am I that I should go to Pharaoh, and bring the Israelites out of Egypt?" 12 [God] said, "I will be with you; and this shall be the sign for you that it is I who sent you: when you have brought the people out of Egypt, you shall worship God on this mountain."

13 But Moses said to God, "If I come to the Israelites and say to them, 'The God of your ancestors has sent me to you,' and they ask me, 'What is his name?' what shall I say to them?" 14 God said to Moses, "I AM WHO I AM." He said further, "Thus you shall say to the Israelites, 'I AM has sent me to you.'" 15 God also said to Moses, "Thus you shall say to the Israelites, 'The LORD, the God of your ancestors, the God of Abraham, the God of Isaac, and the God of Jacob, has sent me to you':

> This is my name forever,
> and this my title for all generations."

Exodus 3:7-15, NRSV

16

Have one person read aloud the Scripture. Have others read silently from different translations and report any differences in the wording.

- How do the differences help you understand the text?

Imagine that you are Moses. You're minding your own business when, out of nowhere, God starts talking to you.

- What would you do?
- What would you say?
- Would you be afraid or intimidated, or would you just talk to God as you would talk to any regular person?
- What, do you think, would God call you to do?

Discuss as a group your answers to these questions.

Then, working in small groups, create a brief dialogue between one of the members of your group and God, using the questions above as a guide. Read or perform your dialogue for the other groups.

- What new insights did you gain by acting out this scenario?

List below any questions you have about the text.

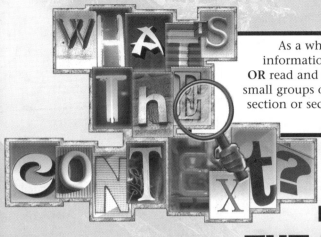

As a whole group, read through this information and discuss the questions; **OR** read and discuss the commentaries in small groups or pairs assigned to a specific section or sections. Then summarize your conversation for the others.

MOSES THE EGYPTIAN

Moses lives in two worlds. He is born an Israelite. But after Pharaoh's daughter shows compassion for him and saves him from the river, he is raised as an Egyptian. In fact, it is Pharaoh's daughter who gives the boy the name *Moses*, which comes from an Egyptian word meaning "to beget a child" and contains the same root as *Thut-mose*, the name of an Egyptian god. Perhaps by coincidence, Moses' name in Hebrew is *Mosheh*, a word derived from the verb *mashah*, which means "to draw out" (as of the water).

In **Acts 7:22**, the martyr Stephen says, "Moses was instructed in all the wisdom of the Egyptians and was powerful in his words and deeds." The Jewish historian Josephus records that Moses was a general in the Egyptian army and conquered Ethiopia. Although Moses integrates into the culture of the Egyptians, he still recognizes his heritage as an Israelite and feels compassion upon seeing the suffering of his people.

- List Moses' character traits, based on what you have read or know. How much do you think Moses knows about himself?
- Do you think that Pharaoh completely accepted Moses as an Egyptian? Explain.
- What about Moses' background prepared him to lead the people out of Egypt? How might this have been part of God's plan?

18

MOSES THE MURDERER

As an adult, Moses visits his Hebrew brothers and sisters; and he sees an Egyptian beating up an Israelite. In a fit of anger, Moses kills the Egyptian. The next day, two Hebrews notice Moses, and one identifies him as the murderer. Moses becomes concerned (rightfully, as it turns out) that his deed will not remain a secret. Once Pharaoh learns of the murder, he puts a bounty on Moses, who escapes to the land of Midian.

Read **Exodus 2:11-22.** Find Midian on an Old Testament map. Now locate Mt. Sinai in relation to Midian.

- What do you think about Moses' act of murder? about his running away?
- Why do you think Pharaoh wants to kill Moses, his adopted grandson?
- Review your list of Moses' character traits. What new insights do these verses give you?
- Where in this Scripture do you see Moses' sense of justice at work? How might this character trait have played a part in God's selection of Moses?

MOSES THE FAMILY MAN

Moses' life as a fugitive provides him an opportunity to marry and start a family. In Midian, Moses protects Reuel's (Jethro's) daughters from shepherds who are trying to keep them from watering their flock (**Exodus 2:16-17**). After this valiant act, Jethro invites Moses to dinner and gives Moses his daughter Zipporah as a wife. Zipporah and Moses have a son, Gershom, which means roughly "alien residing in a foreign land."

Many people, when they move to a new place, settle down, start over, and never look back. It is clear from the name he gives his son that Moses does not forget where he came from. But while Moses lives in Midian, God's people are still in bondage.

- Review your list of Moses' character traits. After looking at Moses' escape to Midian and his family life, what new insights do you have about him?

- Why does Moses help Reuel's daughters? When you consider this incident and his earlier action against the Egyptian, what do you learn about Moses? What do you learn about why God chooses Moses?
- What foreign land do you think Moses is talking about in **Exodus 2:22**? Do you think that Moses is homesick? Explain.
- When have you ever attempted to run away from a difficult situation? What happened?

MOSES THE EXCUSE-MAKER

Before God calls Moses to deliver the people, the people call out to God. Apparently, after the death of Moses' grandfather (Pharaoh), the slave system has become even more oppressive. The Israelites' cry for help reaches God. The events leading up to Moses' call make it seem as though God has been out to lunch concerning the suffering of God's people. After all, they now have been in slavery for almost 400 years.

But God hears the cry of the Israelites. Had the Israelites been calling out before the old king died, or is this the first time? Did God say, "Oh, right, I made a promise to Abraham, Isaac, and Jacob; so let me do something about this situation?" We don't know. We do know that God calls Moses to return to Egypt, and that Moses has plenty of excuses for not going.

Read **Exodus 3:7-15; 4:10-17**.

- Divide into two groups. One group will examine the first section of Scripture (**Exodus 3:7-15**) and the other group will work on the second section (**Exodus 4:10-17**). List the excuses that Moses makes in response to God's call. Restate these excuses in your own words. Then discuss how God reacts to each excuse.
- Given his personality traits, why do you think Moses gives God excuses? Do you think that he feels any guilt for murdering the Egyptian? How might the attitudes of the two Hebrews in **Exodus 2:13-14** have influenced his excuse-making?
- What does God's calling of Moses reveal about God? Consider in your answer the length of time that the Israelites have been slaves.
- When have you felt unqualified for an important task that you were asked to perform? How did you respond?

20

AFTER READING THE TEXT AND THE CONTEXT...

Deal with some or all of these questions before moving to What's Next?

- What new insights do you have?

- What stands out to you in the story now?

- What answers have you gained to questions you raised earlier? What new questions do you have?

- What do you most admire about Moses? What do you least admire?

- What, would you say, are Moses' strengths and weaknesses?

- Why, do you think, does God not choose someone else when Moses makes excuses? What does this say about God?

- Do you think that God really forgot about the Israelites' suffering and the covenant with Abraham? Do you think that the Israelites forgot about God's promises? Explain.

- What does the study text reveal about God and God's relationship with the people of Israel?

- What does the text say about leadership and the character of leaders?

- What one learning will you take from this Scripture and apply to your life?

Choose one or more of Views A, B, and C to discuss; **OR** have different small groups talk about one and then summarize the discussion for the other groups. **Be sure to have everyone complete View U.**

VIEW A — MOSES THE SELLOUT

Have you ever tried to hug a porcupine? It's not easy. Once you try to pick it up, its spines will sink painfully in your skin. For years, Moses had lived the life of the rich and famous. When he went to look upon his Israelite brothers and sisters in bondage, he did not fully understand their plight. And it would have been even harder for the Israelites not to see Moses as a collaborator with the enemy—even after he killed an Egyptian. Moses and his fellow Hebrews lived on different sides of the tracks. The people of Israel do not at first recognize God at work in Moses; instead, they stick their spines in him.

Reread **Exodus 2:11-15.**

- In what ways was Moses separated from his people?
- If you were an Israelite, how would you have viewed Moses? Why? How would Moses' killing of the Egyptian have affected your view of him?
- Why do you think Moses killed the Egyptian? Might he have been angry with himself as well as with the Egyptian? Explain.
- Have you ever been rejected by someone you were trying to help? What happened? How did you feel?
- Have you ever dealt with someone, such as a teacher's pet, whom you and your friends believed was a "collaborator with the enemy"? How did you treat that person? Were you unfair toward that person?

22 VIEW B: MOSES THE INSURRECTIONIST

When you think about it, God calls Moses to be a slave insurrectionist. An insurrectionist is a person who leads a revolt against a government or civil authority. God calls Moses to initiate a revolution—peacefully if possible, but by any means necessary—against the Egyptian government to free the Israelites.

There were also slave insurrectionists during American slavery. Unlike Moses, the slaves were more than willing to lead revolts. The most notable were Denmark Vesey, a member of the African Methodist Episcopal Church; Gabriel Prosser; and Nat Turner. All three of these slaves testified that God told them in a dream to lead their revolts. Turner's revolt was particularly violent. Although these insurrections initially failed, they ultimately contributed to ending the slave system.

- What was at stake politically and economically for the Egyptians when it came to the Hebrew slave system? What was at stake for American colonists when it came to the slave trade?
- What fears do you think an insurrectionist would have? Explain.
- Slave insurrectionists risked not only their lives but those of other slaves, their masters, and the families of both. Was a revolt the right course of action? What other alternatives were available?
- How can people be free spiritually if they are not free politically? Explain.

American slavery had a traumatic effect on those who were enslaved. Willie Lynch, a slave master, wrote a letter on how to destroy slaves' self-esteem to better maintain the slave system. The letter indicated, for example, that slaves should be taught to depend on their masters and to distrust one another. Masters also provoked conflicts between slaves based on gender, age, height, and complexion. How does an insurrectionist arise out of these circumstances? How can people maintain hope and their identity when living in such a system?

- What consequences of American slavery still affect society today? What consequences of slave insurrections still affect us?

 ## SLAVERY STILL

Most people think that slavery ended in the nineteenth century. Not true. Slavery persists (illegally) today in many parts of world. Children in particular often are sold or lured into forced labor or sexual exploits. In Cambodia and Thailand especially, young children are sold as slaves by their families, who are extremely poor and desperate for money. Their "owners" use these children as prostitutes. Many foreign men travel to Southeast Asia to exploit this slave system. Regional governments have been unable (or unwilling) to stop this system.

- What do you know about current-day slavery? How do race, age, gender, and economics factor in to enslavement?
- How does the continued existence of slavery depend on cooperation or support from people who are not directly buying and selling others, such as government officials who look away from the problem or men who travel to these countries and pay to have sex with enslaved children?
- How did American slavery depend on non-slaveholders?
- In what ways other than actual bondage might someone be enslaved?
- How, do you think, does God hear and respond to the cries of enslaved people today? How do you or can you respond to these people's cries?

VIEW: WHO, ME?

The Egyptian and American slave systems were brutal. The trading of child slaves in Asia today is equally sinister and exploitative. In these three examples, we see how governments and economic systems give freedom to some and shackle others.

- Slavery works by lowering the self-esteem of those it oppresses. As you reflect on these systems, what emotions come to your mind? How do you relate to Moses? How do these examples make you feel about your own power to bring about change?
- What forms of "slavery" exist in your community or school? How do you feel God calling you to fight for justice? What excuses have you given God?
- Write your reflections on this question: How can you and the church make a difference in systems that oppress individuals and groups because of gender, race, or class?
- Read **Galatians 3:28.** How does this verse affect your understanding of how people are divided by legal, social, or economic status today? How have you experienced your Christian faith overcoming such separations?
- How do personal prejudices help maintain enslaving systems? How are those prejudices developed? Pray that God will remove any prejudices from your spirit.

Check *www.ileadyouth.com/3V*
for worship suggestions.

LET MY PEOPLE GO

Exodus 11:4-10; 12:29-32

During slavery in America, slaves would sing spirituals to give themselves hope. They also used spirituals to communicate messages about escapes or other subversive activities in a way that slave masters would not understand. One such spiritual, "Go Down, Moses," repeated the line, "Let my people go." The song uses the Exodus story to depict the sullen spirit of the slave and the slave's longing for justice and freedom. To American slaves, the story of Moses and the Israelites was a message of hope from God.

26

4 Moses said, "Thus says the LORD: About midnight I will go out through Egypt. 5 Every firstborn in the land of Egypt shall die, from the firstborn of Pharaoh who sits on his throne to the firstborn of the female slave who is behind the handmill, and all the firstborn of the livestock. 6 Then there will be a loud cry throughout the whole land of Egypt, such as has never been or will ever be again. 7 But not a dog shall growl against any of the Israelites—not at people, not at animals—so that you may know that the LORD makes a distinction between Egypt and Israel. 8 Then all these officials of yours shall come down to me, and bow low to me, saying, 'Leave us, you and all the people who follow you.' After that I will leave." And in hot anger he left Pharaoh.

9 The LORD said to Moses, "Pharaoh will not listen to you, in order that my wonders may be multiplied in the land of Egypt." 10 Moses and Aaron performed all these wonders before Pharaoh; but the LORD hardened Pharaoh's heart, and he did not let the people of Israel go out of his land.

. . . .

29 At midnight the LORD struck down all the firstborn in the land of Egypt, from the firstborn of Pharaoh who sat on his throne to the firstborn of the prisoner who was in the dungeon, and all the firstborn of the livestock. 30 Pharaoh arose in the night, he and all his officials and all the Egyptians; and there was a loud cry in Egypt, for there was not a house without someone dead. 31 Then he summoned Moses and Aaron in the night, and said, "Rise up, go away from among my people, both you and the Israelites! Go worship the LORD, as you said. 32 Take your flocks and your herds, as you have said, and be gone. And bring a blessing on me too!"

Exodus 11:4-10; 12:29-32, NRSV

Read the passage aloud.

- What questions does the text raise for you?

Highlight any words or phrases that you feel are important.

Imagine that you are a news reporter in Egypt on the night of the first Passover. What would your report include? What, do you think, would eyewitnesses tell you? What sounds and sights would you expect to find? Have everyone in your group create notes for a news report to present to the others.

As a whole group, read through this information and discuss the questions; **OR** read and discuss the commentaries in small groups or pairs assigned to a specific section or sections. Then summarize your conversation for the others.

SIGNS AND WONDERS

When God asks him to return to Egypt, Moses makes the excuse that no one would listen to him or believe that God had sent him. Moses wasn't referring to the Egyptians alone, but also to his own people. After all, the Israelites had been slaves for four hundred years.

- Why would God suddenly act after doing nothing for so long?
- Do you think that God ignored the Israelites' suffering? Or did they ignore God? Explain.
- Why would God send an Egyptian prince and runaway outlaw who had never endured the hardships the Israelites had suffered?

God answers Moses' objection by providing three "signs and wonders" for Moses to perform so that the Israelites will believe that God sent him. They even rehearse the wonders together so that Moses will have them down pat. Read **Exodus 4:1-9** and list these signs.

God also gives the stuttering Moses a spokesperson, his brother Aaron. Read **Exodus 4:27-31** to learn what happens after Moses and Aaron meet in the wilderness and go to Egypt.

- Why do the Israelites need signs and wonders in order to believe?
- What does it take to make you believe that God is calling you or acting through events?
- What does the necessity of signs and wonders suggest about how the Israelites may have felt about Moses? What does it suggest about how they may have felt about God?

WHAT DOES GOD WANT?

Because Exodus tells the story of the Israelites' liberation from slavery, we assume that Moses is talking about his people's journey to freedom when he tells Pharaoh, "Let my people go." Actually, God's initial demand is much more modest.

Read **Exodus 5:1-5** and write down what Moses and Aaron ask Pharaoh to do.

- How does Pharaoh react? Are you surprised by his reaction?
- Why would Pharaoh not allow the Israelites to leave Egyptian supervision to celebrate a festival to God?

During American slavery, slave-owners were as distrusting of their slaves as Pharaoh was of the Israelites. Masters wanted their slaves to be Christians yet were deeply suspicious about the religious meetings (sometimes called "shouts") that slaves held at night, when they would sing spirituals and hear preaching from fellow slaves (often about Moses and the Exodus!).

- Why would masters want their slaves to be Christians?
- Why would slaveholders be concerned about allowing slaves to practice religion?
- Many states made it a crime to teach slaves to read and write. Why would the master class want slaves to be uneducated?
- What similarities do you notice between Pharaoh and American slaveholders? between the Israelites and American slaves? What differences do you notice?

LET MY PEOPLE GO ... GOING ONCE

Egypt has had several Pharaohs since Joseph lived in the land. The Pharaoh in our story may only have *heard* of Moses but never met him. And when Moses demands that Pharaoh let the Hebrews go because the Lord said so, Pharaoh has no clue about who the "LORD" is. The Egyptians worshiped many gods and believed that Pharaoh himself was a deity. Not surprisingly, Pharaoh refuses to recognize God's authority.

Read **Exodus 5:1-9** to learn Pharaoh's response when Moses initially presents God's demand.

- In what ways can you relate to Pharaoh?
- Why does Pharaoh refuse to let the Hebrew people go?
- What does he do instead? Why do you think he responds this way? How would you have responded if you were Pharaoh?
- In what way does Pharaoh keep his own people in bondage?
- The Israelites were responsible for building Egypt's great storage cities of Rameses and Pithom (see **Exodus 1:8-12**). Why do you think Pharaoh refers to them as lazy?

Prior to the Civil War, four million African-American slaves lived in the United States. They provided much of the labor supply from Maryland to Texas to Missouri to Florida. (In the seventeenth and eighteenth centuries, slave labor also prevailed in northern cities, such as New York.)

- Why, do you think, were masters, like Pharaoh, so reluctant to free their slaves and simply hire them as freed laborers?
- Why would American slave masters and Pharaoh commonly believe that slaves were lazy?
- Why do you think free people in slave states were afraid of being outnumbered by slaves, as the Egyptians were afraid?
- How can calling people derogatory names affect their self-esteem? How does low self-esteem keep people in bondage?

LET MY PEOPLE GO EIGHT MORE TIMES

The second time Moses and Aaron visit Pharaoh, the Egyptian ruler demands a sign from their God. Aaron, following God's instructions, throws down his staff, which turns into a snake. Pharaoh's sorcerers, longtime practitioners of magic, aren't impressed. They throw down their own staffs, which also turn into snakes. At least the magicians aren't impressed until Aaron's snake swallows up theirs. Even so, as God had told Moses, Pharaoh's heart is hardened. When Moses returns, he promises Pharaoh that God will send plagues unless the Israelites are freed. It takes ten plagues before Pharaoh, who disregards his own people's safety, gets the message.

Below, list the first nine plagues and the consequences of each:

First Plague (Exodus 7:14-25)

Second Plague (Exodus 8:1-15)

Third Plague (Exodus 8:16-19)

Fourth Plague (Exodus 8:20-32)

Fifth Plague (Exodus 9:1-7)

Sixth Plague (Exodus 9:8-12)

Seventh Plague (Exodus 9:13-35)

Eighth Plague (Exodus 10:12-20)

Ninth Plague (Exodus 10:21-29)

32

A HARDENED HEART

Pharaoh's responses to the signs and wonders and the plagues brought on by God through Moses and Aaron follow a pattern. Often, Pharaoh relents to Moses' demands—he even asks Moses to pray for him and admits that he has sinned against God—only to change his mind and refuse to let the Israelites go. Exodus consistently uses the same phrase to describe Pharaoh's reversal: His heart was hardened.

Read about Pharaoh's "hardened heart" in the verses listed below:

- Exodus 7:3-4
- Exodus 8:8-15
- Exodus 9:10-12
- Exodus 7:14
- Exodus 8:19
- Exodus 9:27-35
- Exodus 7:20-23
- Exodus 8:25-32
- Exodus 10:1-2

Read these passages carefully and you'll notice that sometimes the texts say that Pharaoh is to blame for his hardened heart and sometimes they say that God hardens Pharaoh's heart.

- Who do you think is responsible for Pharaoh's hardened heart? Is Pharaoh merely God's instrument, or is he acting of his own free will? Explain.
- Why would God harden Pharaoh's heart? Why wouldn't God, instead, soften Pharaoh's heart so that God's people could be freed?
- What does it mean to have a hardened heart?
- Where do you see hardened hearts today in our society?
- When has your heart been hardened? Who or what hardened it?

THE TENTH PLAGUE: THE ULTIMATUM

Although the first nine plagues seriously affect Egypt and its people, the final one hits Pharaoh directly. After the death of every firstborn Egyptian, including Pharaoh's son, the grieving king begs the Israelites to leave. He even asks for a blessing on their way out.

The Israelites depart with much more than the clothes on their backs. Following God's instructions to Moses, they ask their Egyptian neighbors for objects of silver and gold. After the final plague, the Egyptians are only too willing to give up their fine jewelry and clothing, since they fear that the Israelites will only bring further death and destruction (**Exodus 12:33-36**). (*Pay attention in the later Bible studies in this book to learn what happens to all of this wealth!*)

- The account of the last plague is packed with violence. List the violent acts associated with this last plague. Who is being violent to whom? For what purpose? Who is ultimately responsible?
- What does this plague suggest about God's character? What does it suggest about the fight for freedom?
- Why does Pharaoh ask Moses and Aaron for a blessing?
- Reread **Exodus 1:22**. How does Pharaoh's order to kill Israelite boys contribute to your understanding of the final plague against Egypt? to your understanding of who is ultimately responsible for the plague?
- If God's purpose is freeing Israel, why do you think God sanctions the escaping Israelites plundering of their Egyptian neighbors?

34

AFTER READING THE TEXT AND THE CONTEXT...

Deal with some or all of these questions before moving to What's Next?

- What new insights do you have?

- What answers have you gained to questions you raised earlier?

- How has Moses' character changed as he has gone from the runaway excuse-maker to the leader who confronts Pharaoh?

- What significance does God's protection of the Israelites—symbolized by the Passover—have for the freedom of God's people today?

- Is God violent? Justify your answer.

- How is God responsible for inflicting upon the Egyptians plagues and the deaths of so many people and animals? How are Pharaoh and the Egyptians responsible?

- The American Civil War and the Emancipation Proclamation ultimately ended slavery in the United States. What are the consequences of overthrowing a system like slavery? How do these consequences help a nation? How do they hurt?

- What one learning will you take from this Scripture and apply to your life?

Choose one or more of Views A, B, and C to discuss; **OR** have different small groups talk about one and then summarize the discussion for the other groups. **Be sure to have everyone complete View U.**

WHAT GOES AROUND ...

Maybe you've heard the phrases "What goes around comes around" and "If you can't take it, don't dish it out." Sometimes we don't consider that how we treat others will come back around to us. In some cases, how our grandparents treated others can even come back either to bless or haunt us. Pharaoh of this story, whose eldest son died in the final plague, suffered the consequences of policies begun by the two pharaohs before him.

- Who do you think was most responsible for the plagues on Egypt? Pharaoh? The two previous pharaohs? Both of the above? God? Explain.
- When have the consequences of something you did (good or bad) come back around to you. How did you feel?
- How are people today paying for or benefiting from the actions of earlier generations? In what ways do future generations reap the consequences of alcoholism, drug abuse, or domestic violence?
- Read **Galatians 6:1-10.** How does the law of reaping and sowing relate to your answer to the question above?
- How does the story of the Israelites relate to forgiveness and loving enemies? How do the plagues against Egypt fit with these biblical principles? Are those principles even applicable when people are oppressed and not free to worship? Must violence beget violence?
- Read **Romans 12:9-21.** How does this Scripture affect your views on forgiveness, vengeance, and violence?
- Read **Exodus 20:4-6.** How does this passage affect your answers to the above questions?

THE PASSOVER

Before bringing the disastrous final plague on Egypt, God institutes the Passover and teaches Moses how the Israelites and their descendants should remember an event that has not yet even occurred. The instructions on celebrating Passover are highly detailed.

More than 3,000 years later, Jews around the world continue to celebrate Passover as a time to recall God's delivering them from oppression in Egypt and God's faithfulness to the promises made to Abraham, Isaac, and Jacob. During other times of trial and persecution—the Exile in Babylon, the harsh Greek and Roman rule, the Spanish Inquisition, and even the Holocaust—celebrating Passover as a community has helped Jewish people remember that God hears their cries and will remain faithful to God's promise.

- Does your family or culture have traditional celebrations commemorating special events? How do family and cultural traditions offer us hope and encouragement? How are you strengthened by these celebrations?

On the night of his arrest, Jesus institutes the Lord's Supper during a Passover meal. Jesus became the sacrificial lamb.

- How does the use of lamb's blood during Passover take on a new or different meaning with the Lord's Supper, or Holy Communion?
- How do you interpret Jesus' sacrifice in terms of the promise of deliverance at the original Passover?
- Read **Romans 7:14-15**. How does Jesus free you from slavery to be one of God's people?

VIEW C: RESPONDING TO OPPRESSION

During American slavery, slaves found many different ways to respond to their bondage. Some ran away. A few led violent rebellions. Many resisted by slowing down the pace of work or even sabotaging farm equipment. And many cooperated with their masters—often because they saw no alternative and sought to make the best of the situation.

The same divisions were apparent among the Israelites. Read in **Exodus 5:15-21** how some Hebrew slaves respond to Moses just after his first confrontation with Pharaoh.

- Dr. Martin Luther King, Jr., and Mahatma Gandhi were leaders who taught nonviolent resistance as a means of securing civil rights for all in the United States and India, respectively. Others seeking rights believed that violence was necessary to accomplish their goals. How do God's actions in this story shine light this debate?

- How does the situation faced by the Israelites in Egypt compare with those faced by King and Gandhi?

DELIVERING DELIVERANCE

God's actions in Egypt are not only a deliverance; they are also an example and a calling.

After the Israelites have fled Egypt, God tells them repeatedly, "Once you settle in the Promised Land, do not oppress foreigners who live among you; if you do, I will hear their cries, just as I heard yours in Egypt."

Read **Exodus 23:9**; **Leviticus 19:33-34**; and **Deuteronomy 10:19** for examples of God's directive. God not only says, "Love your neighbor as yourself" (**Leviticus 19:18**) but to love the foreigners among you as your neighbors.

Jesus' teaching on this subject—the parable of the good Samaritan (**Luke 10:29-37**)—also ends with a directive: Go and do as the Samaritan (a foreigner) did for the man who had been attacked by robbers. We are to respond to God's deliverance by delivering others and hearing the cries of those in need.

- In what ways today are people "enslaved"?
- Where and when do you encounter people in need of deliverance?
- How are you treating the "foreigners" in your community?
- How are you responding to the cries of those in need?

Check www.ileadyouth.com/3V for worship suggestions.

HOW DO YOU GET WATER FROM A ROCK?

Exodus 17:1-7

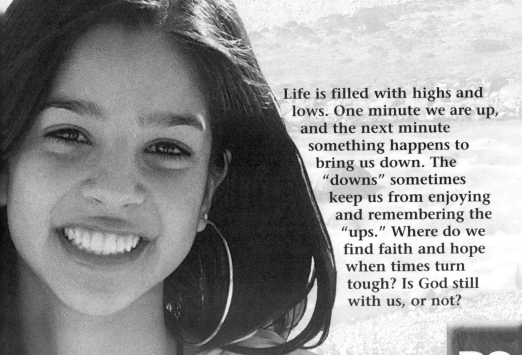

Life is filled with highs and lows. One minute we are up, and the next minute something happens to bring us down. The "downs" sometimes keep us from enjoying and remembering the "ups." Where do we find faith and hope when times turn tough? Is God still with us, or not?

40

¹ From the wilderness of Sin the whole congregation of the Israelites journeyed by stages, as the LORD commanded. They camped at Rephidim, but there was no water for the people to drink. ² The people quarreled with Moses, and said, "Give us water to drink." Moses said to them, "Why do you quarrel with me? Why do you test the LORD?" 3 But the people thirsted there for water; and the people complained against Moses, and said, "Why did you bring us out of Egypt, to kill us and our children and livestock with thirst?" 4 So Moses cried out to the LORD, "What shall I do with this people? They are almost ready to stone me." 5 The LORD said to Moses, "Go on ahead of the people, and take some of the elders of Israel with you; take in your hand the staff with which you struck the Nile, and go. 6 I will be standing there in front of you on the rock at Horeb. Strike the rock, and water will come out of it, so that the people may drink." Moses did so in the sight of the elders of Israel. 7 He called the place Massah and Meribah, because the Israelites quarreled and tested the LORD, saying, "Is the LORD among us or not?"

Exodus 17:1-7, NRSV

Have someone read the passage aloud while others read silently from different versions. Report any differences in the wording. How do the differences add to your understanding of the text?

Highlight words or phrases in the text that you feel are important. Make a list of questions that the text raises for you.

On a markerboard or large sheet of paper, list the characters in this story. Beside each character's name, write words that describe that character's emotions.

Form three groups of volunteers to stage brief skits depicting 1) the Israelites' conversation with Moses; 2) Moses' conversation with God; and 3) the Israelites' response to the water coming from the rock.

- What insights about the Scripture did you gain from this exercise?
- What new questions do you have?
- What, do you think, was at the root of the Israelites' complaints? Why would some of them feel abandoned by God?

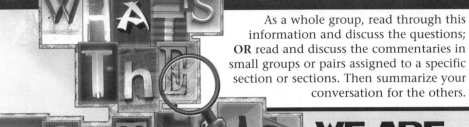

> As a whole group, read through this information and discuss the questions; OR read and discuss the commentaries in small groups or pairs assigned to a specific section or sections. Then summarize your conversation for the others.

WE ARE ABOUT TO DIE

In reading the story of the Israelites' delivery from Egypt, we're struck by Pharaoh's stubbornness. Even after ten devastating plagues, Pharaoh seems not to understand what kind of God he's dealing with. And yet the children of Israel are no better than Pharaoh.

As a miraculous pillar of cloud by day and fire by night, God leads the Israelites away from Egypt and to the Sea of Reeds. Yet when the people see Pharaoh's army pursuing them, they stop trusting God and tell Moses that they would have been better off remaining as slaves in Egypt. Read some of this memorable exchange in **Exodus 14:10-14**.

When God parts the sea and delivers the Israelites, they again sing God's praises and regain their trust in God. But almost as soon as they enter the wilderness of Sinai, they begin complaining all over again.

Read **Exodus 15:22-25** and **16:1-8**.

- In these two Scriptures why do the Israelites complain?
- What do their complaints reveal about their faith in God?
- In each case, how does God respond to the people's complaints?
- Why do you think the people still have trouble trusting God?
- Perhaps you've heard the old saying, "Better the devil you know than the devil you don't know." How do the Israelites' attitudes reflect this saying?
- When have you ever wished for the "devil you know," instead of having to face a new, uncertain situation?

THE SCENIC ROUTE

There was a much more direct way for the Israelites to travel from Egypt to the Promised Land of Canaan than through the Sinai wilderness. They could have traveled a well established route along the Mediterranean cost. But instead, God leads them on "the scenic route"—down one side of the Sinai Peninsula and back up the other, with a notable stop at Mt. Sinai (or Horeb) along the way.

Use a Bible map to locate Egypt, Canaan, the route that scholars believe the Israelites took through the wilderness, and the more direct route available along the coast.

Notice that the direct route would have led the Israelites into the land of the Philistines—the people who would become Israel's fiercest enemy.

- Why do you think God kept the Israelites away from the Philistines?
- How might the Israelites' track record of trust in God (or lack thereof) have been a factor in God's choice of routes?
- Why, do you think, would God later decree that everyone among the Israelites who had left Egypt would have to die before their children and grandchildren could enter the Promised Land?

HEY, GOD, WHAT HAVE YOU DONE FOR US LATELY?

Had it been available in his time, Moses might have displayed in his tent one of the popular workplace posters that reads, "It's hard to soar with eagles when you work with turkeys." At times, Moses, who was old enough to be retired and enjoying the good life, must have wondered how he ended up leading a complaining nation of Israelites.

Even after witnessing their miraculous delivery from Pharaoh's army, God's people still don't have faith that God will provide for them. In fact, they seem to do more complaining in the wilderness than they had done in slavery. Although they have God's pillar of fire to lead them, they still ask, "Is the LORD among us or not?" (**Exodus 17:7**). Amid their doubt, they become angry enough to kill Moses.

Moses understands that his people's real complaint is not with him but with God. "Why do you quarrel with me?" he asks. "Why do you test the LORD?" (**Exodus 17:2**).

- Why, do you think, do the Israelites complain so much after all that God has done for them?
- Why, do you think, do the Israelites take their frustrations on out on Moses, instead of on God?
- What does Moses mean when he asks, "Why do you test the LORD?"
- How, do you think, has the four hundred years of slavery that the Israelites had endured affected their faith in God?

Read **Hebrews 11:1.** When the Israelites go through trials in the wilderness, they remind Moses how good they had it in Egypt. They had depended on the Egyptians for everything, and the Egyptians had depended on them for labor.

- What is God teaching the Israelites in the desert? Why is God's lesson so difficult to teach?
- Why must the Israelites learn this lesson to live freely as God's people?

WHO WERE THE ELDERS?

In giving Moses a solution to the lack of water, God tells him to go ahead of the people and take some of the elders with him. In the Jewish tradition, the elders were older men in the community, leaders who held the Law for the Jewish nation. For example, the prophets would receive the Law from God and, in turn, give the Law to the elders. Today, we refer to pastors or ministers in the church as elders. God wants these religious leaders to witness the miracle of the water coming from the rock in the desert.

- Why, do you think, does God want the elders to witness this miracle?
- In this Scripture, why would it be important to have all of the Israelites' leaders on the same page?
- In addition to pastors, who are the "elders" in the church today?

Read **James 5:13-15.**

- How do these verses affect your understanding of the role of elders in our churches?

WHO WAS THE ROCK?

God addresses the Israelites' question, "Is the LORD among us or not?" by producing water from the rock. Scientific research shows that water can indeed spring from rocks. And the rock at Horeb represents more than just a water fountain; there is enough water to quench the thirst of the whole nation for a long period of time. The "rock" was God's power first revealed in Creation and ultimately through the life and resurrection of Jesus.

- What is the significance of Moses hitting the rock once to bring forth water? Why doesn't God bring forth the water without having Moses do anything?
- How does your faith in God free you to reach your full potential in God? How does living without faith hold a person in bondage and limit his or her life's choices?

Read **1 Corinthians 10:1-6.**

- In your own words describe what Paul thought about the protections God sent to the Israelites to ease their fears. What specifically does he say about the rock at Horeb? For Paul, who was the rock?
- In what ways is Jesus the "rock"?

Read **John 4:10-14.**

- In what way is Jesus the "water"?

Read **Numbers 20:1-13**, the story of a second time the Israelites receive water from a rock.

- In this Scripture how does Moses fail to trust God?
- What punishment do he and Aaron receive? Do you think that the punishment is fair? Explain.
- What role does obedience play in being free to be God's people?

46

AFTER READING THE TEXT AND THE CONTEXT...

Deal with some or all of these questions before moving to What's Next?

- What new insights do you have?

- What answers to earlier questions did you find?

- How do you see yourself in any of the characters in this Scripture?

- How does knowing that Moses will not see the Promised Land affect your view of him? (See **Numbers 20:1-13**.)

- Do you think that the Israelites were disrespectful in their treatment of Moses? Why, or why not?

- How do you participate in your own miracles? How do you participate in miracles that others experience? In what ways have you had to "hit some rocks"?

- What does this text say to you about leadership and obedience?

- In what ways has God protected you?

- When do you feel like asking, "Is the LORD among us or not?"

- What one learning will you take from this Scripture and apply to your life?

Choose one or more of Views A, B, and C to discuss; OR have different small groups talk about one and then summarize the discussion for the other groups. **Be sure to have everyone complete View U.**

WHEN CRISIS COMES

We all ride emotional roller coasters sometimes. One day we can be elated because we made an *A* on a test or earned a starting spot on the school soccer team. The next day we can feel low because we did poorly on another test, which we had expected to ace, or had a heated argument with a best friend. We forget all about the joy of the previous day and can focus only on the stress and worry of the moment.

The Israelites in the desert were just the same. Whenever a new challenge arose—lack of water, shortage of food—they quickly lost faith in God, who had done so much for them and brought them so far.

It's hard to have the faith to stay positive when times are tough. But God wants us to have the kind of faith that can endure letdowns and crises, because such faith can be truly liberating.

• How does your faith make you free?

Think of a crisis that you have faced. Which of the responses below would best describe how you react to a crisis situation?

- Panic
- Tell everybody about the situation
- Dwell on negative thoughts
- Take your own advice
- Become fearful
- Read the Bible
- Pray
- Another alternative

Read **Philippians 4:4-7**—verses that Paul wrote while imprisoned, facing what most of us would consider a crisis situation.

• How does this Scripture add to your understanding of being freed to be God's people?

48

VIEW B: OUT OF EGYPT, STILL IN BONDAGE

"You can take a boy out of the country," goes the old saying, "but you can't take the country out of the boy." The "country," in this case, represents more than a geographic location; it is a way of life and a mindset that does not easily change.

Moses kept running up against such a mindset among the Israelites. He could take them out of Egypt, but he couldn't take the Egypt out of them. More than four hundred years of servitude had given them a slave mentality. They were conditioned to work for and depend on others. They remained in bondage spiritually and mentally. They were not ready to enter the Promised Land.

- How do certain habits or ways of thinking become addictive? How can they limit one's ability to live fully as a Christian?
- What material things hold you "in bondage"?
- In what ways is remaining in bondage easier than facing new challenges? How does God call you to move from bondage to freedom?

Read **Romans 7:21–8:2.**

- How is sin a form of slavery?
- How does being "in Christ" free us from slavery?
- The apostle Paul sometimes refers to himself as a slave to Christ? What do you think he means?

LEADERSHIP HAS ITS PRICE

In the movie *A Bug's Life*, the grasshopper tells the ants' young queen-in-training something that Moses could relate to: "The first rule of leadership? It's all your fault."

Being the leader of an organization, a facilitator of a study group, a big brother or sister, a church youth group president, a committee chair, or a team captain can be an overwhelming responsibility. It may require you to spend much of your time putting out fires that others have started. On top of that, being a leader is a thankless job. People complain. They give you grief. They blame you for things you didn't do. Remember that the higher you are, the more people can see you. And high visibility can make you an easier target.

- Do you think that some people are born leaders? Or do they get to the top by hard work, luck, or knowing the right people? Explain.
- List some qualities that you look for in a leader. Which do you regard as most important?
- How important do you think it is for leaders to take care of themselves as they serve others? What are the dangers of this philosophy?
- In what ways do you think leaders are sometimes treated unfairly?
- Why would anyone want to be a leader?

 **THE BLAME GAME**

The Israelites blame Moses when they find themselves without water. Moses points out that their issue is really with God.

We also often blame others when we run into difficult situations. We blame our parents, siblings, friends, or others when bad things that are beyond our control happen to us. We blame those around us whom we can see, instead of taking our worries, frustrations, and fears to God.

Take time to think about what is going in your life that you need to turn over to God in prayer and meditation.

Write your reflections about the following question:

- How will turning these parts of my life over to God free me spiritually?

Check www.ileadyouth.com/3V
for worship suggestions.

FREEDOM HAS A PRICE

Exodus 20:1-20

As a teenager trying to assert your independence, exercising your newfound freedom can be difficult. We have rules at school, rules at home, rules in society, and even rules in the church. How can a person live freely with so many rules?

¹ Then God spoke all these words:

² I am the LORD your God, who brought you out of the land of Egypt, out of the house of slavery; ³ you shall have no other gods before me.

⁴ You shall not make for yourself an idol, whether in the form of anything that is in heaven above, or that is on the earth beneath, or that is in the water under the earth. ⁵ You shall not bow down to them or worship them; for I the LORD your God am a jealous God, punishing children for the iniquity of parents, to the third and fourth generation of those who reject me, ⁶ but showing steadfast love to the thousandth generation of those who love me and keep my commandments.

⁷ You shall not make wrongful use of the name of the LORD your God, for the LORD will not acquit anyone who misuses his name.

⁸ Remember the sabbath day, to keep it holy. ⁹ Six days you shall labor and do all your work. ¹⁰ But the seventh day is a sabbath to the LORD your God; you shall not do any work—you, your son or your daughter, your male or female slave, your livestock, or the alien resident in your towns. ¹¹ For in six days the LORD made heaven and earth, the sea, and all that is in them, but rested the seventh day; therefore the LORD blessed the sabbath day and consecrated it.

¹² Honor your father and your mother, so that your days may be long in the land that the LORD your God is giving you.

¹³ You shall not murder.

¹⁴ You shall not commit adultery.

¹⁵ You shall not steal.

¹⁶ You shall not bear false witness against your neighbor.

¹⁷ You shall not covet your neighbor's house; you shall not covet your neighbor's wife, or male or female slave, or ox, or donkey, or anything that belongs to your neighbor.

¹⁸ When all the people witnessed the thunder and lightning, the sound of the trumpet, and the mountain smoking, they were afraid and trembled and stood at a distance, ¹⁹ and said to Moses, "You speak to us, and we will listen; but let not God speak to us, or we will die." ²⁰ Moses said to the people, "Do not be afraid; for God has come only to test you and to put the fear of him upon you so that you do not sin."

Exodus 20:1-20, NRSV

Read the passage aloud. What are your initial reactions to the text?

- Highlight words or phrases you consider important.
- What questions does the text raise for you?
- In what tone does God hand down this list of rules? How does the thunder and the smoke affect your answer?
- Are these ten rules simply a new form of slavery? Explain.
- How could obeying someone's rules lead to freedom?

Divide into small groups. Assign one or more commandments to each group. Ask the members to discuss and explain to everyone what they think their assigned commandments mean. What did they mean when they were given? Do they have added or different meanings today?

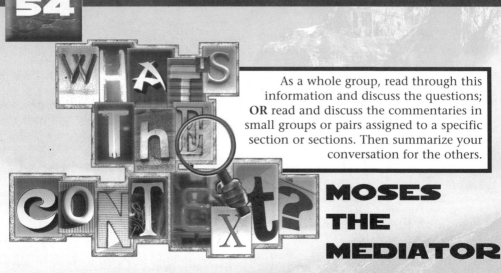

WHAT'S THE CONTEXT?

As a whole group, read through this information and discuss the questions; **OR** read and discuss the commentaries in small groups or pairs assigned to a specific section or sections. Then summarize your conversation for the others.

MOSES THE MEDIATOR

During their journey to freedom, the Israelites never have a one-on-one conversation with God. Instead, Moses acts as their mediator. Mostly, Moses listens as God gives commands for the Israelites to follow. After moving through the wilderness, the people camp in front of Mt. Sinai, while God stays atop the mountain.

Moses' exchanges with God take place in **Exodus 19.** God instructs Moses to tell the Israelites that their obedience is necessary for them to be considered God's people (verses 4-6). In a second conversation, God tells Moses to consecrate the people in preparation for God's appearance (verses 9b-15). God emphasizes that if the people look upon God, they will die. Only Moses can look upon God. When God appears to the people, with the top of the mountain surrounded in fire and a cloud of smoke, Moses hears God speak in thunder. God makes it clear that Moses is the Israelites' representative to God.

- What do the limitations that God places on the Israelites say about God's character? Why do you think God makes these restrictions?
- Why does God never come down from the mountain or let the people come up? What does this say about God? about us?
- Why, do you think, would looking at God kill a person?
- What pressures might Moses have felt as his people's link to God? How does Moses' role compare with that of a pastor in a church?
- Moses interprets God's thunder, but the other Israelites cannot. What does this say about how God speaks to us? Can you understand thunder? Explain.
- How do you sometimes hear God's voice?

GOD SPOKE THESE WORDS

Now read **Exodus 19:20-25.** God calls Moses to the mountain a third time and emphasizes that no one (aside from Moses and Aaron, whom God instructs Moses to bring along on the next trip up the mountain) should come around the mountain. God intends to keep the mountain holy.

When God speaks again, Moses receives the Ten Commandments, or Decalogue (from the Greek prefix for "ten" and the Greek word *logos,* which means "word"). Through Moses the people hear that, to remain in covenant with God, God requires obedience to certain laws.

- God set limits around the mountain to keep it holy. Why do you think God believes that the people will defile the mountain?
- Why is keeping the mountain holy necessary? How does your answer relate to the events that take place on the mountain?
- When the Israelites leave slavery under Pharaoh, they are under the authority of God, who likewise demands their obedience. What is the difference between being under Pharaoh's rule and being under God's rule?
- What risks do the Israelites face in their new situation if they fail to obey God?
- Why do you think God gives the Israelites the Ten Commandments? In what ways do the commandments limit freedom? How do they promote freedom?

THE LORD YOUR GOD

One reason Moses was reluctant to answer God's call was that he did not know what to call God. When he asked God's name, God replied, "I AM WHO I AM" (sometimes translated "I will be who I will be").

In the ancient world, knowing someone's name (or bestowing a name on someone) meant holding a certain power over that person. God, by not revealing the divine name, made a point. To this day, many Jewish people follow the ancient custom of rendering God's name as YHWH (the first letters of the Hebrew words for "I am who I am") or in English leaving a blank (G_d) instead of fully spelling God's name.

But Moses also had a valid point. After all, he told God, people have to call you *something*. Will they believe that you're legitimate if you won't even reveal your identity? Read this exchange in **Exodus 3:13-15**.

So God commanded Moses to tell the people, "The LORD, the God of your ancestors, the God of Abraham, the God of Isaac, and the God of Jacob, has sent me to you" (**Exodus 3:15**).

At the beginning of the Decalogue, God says, "I am the LORD your God who brought you out of the land of Egypt, out of the house of slavery." Note the change in emphasis. God shifts from the "God of Abraham, God of Isaac, the God of Jacob" to being *their* God, because God has delivered them from slavery. Scholars believe that this commandment comes first in the Decalogue because it commands a belief in God's existence. God is not simply "a god" of our dead ancestors, but a living God who is active in our lives.

- How did God's deliverance of them from Egypt create a more personal relationship between God and the Israelites?
- Here, God wants to be defined as the God of deliverance. How, do you think, did the Israelites define God at this point in their journey? Why?
- Why is recognizing God's authority a prerequisite to obeying the remainder of the commandments?
- To the Israelites, what was the source of God's authority?
- How do you recognize God's authority in your life?

THE RELATIONSHIP WITH GOD THROUGH GOD

The first four commandments center on maintaining a holy relationship with God: 1) Acknowledge God's authority. 2) Neither make nor worship images of God. (God cannot be made by human hands.) 3) Do not misuse God's name or make false oaths invoking God. 4) Keep the sabbath day holy.

These four mandates reiterate God's sovereignty. The Hebrew people are to worship and revere God alone. In delivering them from Egypt, God claimed them. They are God's people.

- Review these commandments. How does each relate to worship and respect?

Reread **Exodus 20:4-6**. These commandments concern making images of God. Unlike many of the other commandments, God inserts some additional commentary.

- What does God's warning reveal about God? What does it reveal about the sins of our ancestors? about us?

To traditional Jews, making even a reverent image of God—as in Michelangelo's famous painting of Creation on the ceiling of the Sistine Chapel in Rome—is blasphemous.

- What do you think of this view of the second commandment? Do these verses mean that it is wrong to wear a cross? Explain.

Reread **Exodus 20:7**.

- What does this verse mean to you? List some ways this law might be broken. Read **Matthew 12:31-32** and **Mark 3:28-29**. Is Jesus referring to this commandment? Why do you think blaspheming the Holy Spirit is an unforgivable sin? Can't all sins be forgiven?

Reread **Exodus 20:8-11**.

- What information does God add to this commandment?
- What does sabbath mean to you? How do you keep the sabbath holy? Why would this be so important to God?

THE RELATIONSHIP WITH GOD THROUGH OTHERS

The remaining six commandments concentrate on our relationships with other people. God reveals that being obedient to God requires us to treat other people with the same respect as we treat God. Through these commandments, God stresses the importance of love for one another. Jesus reiterates this emphasis in his teaching.

- How, do you think, does loving God relate to loving others?
- Read **1 John 4:7-12.** How does this passage affect your understanding of the relationship between loving God and loving neighbor? Now read **1 John 2:7.** How is this verse "no new commandment?"

We often render the commandment dealing with murder as "You shall not kill." However, the Hebrew Scriptures distinguish between murder and killing. Read **Exodus 20:14; Leviticus 20:10;** and **Deuteronomy 22:23-24.**

- How do you interpret these two commandments?
- What if any distinction do you make between murder and other killing? Why? How does your understanding of Jesus' teachings affect your answer? How do your reflections on the Israelites' escape from Pharaoh's army affect your answer?
- Why, do you think, is avoiding adultery among the Ten Commandments? Why is the suggested punishment so severe? Why would society not impose such a punishment today?

Reread **Exodus 20:15.** This commandment appears in almost every penal code around the world. Some scholars have interpreted this commandment as a prohibition against kidnapping because there are many other Hebrew laws against the stealing of property.

- In what ways do you think the Ten Commandments have influenced our societal codes in both civil law (wrongs against people) and criminal law?

AFTER READING THE TEXT AND THE CONTEXT...

Deal with some or all of these questions before moving to What's Next?

- What new insights do you have?

- What answers to questions you raised earlier did you gain?

- In what ways do you identify with the Israelites in this Scripture?

- What does this text say about obedience, fear, and authority?

- Does God deal with people on an individual basis? How do you communicate with God? How does God communicate with you individually?

- Are the Israelites operating out of fear of God, faith in God, or both?

- How can you "understand thunder"?

- What one learning will you take from this Scripture and apply to your life?

Choose one or more of Views A, B, and C to discuss; **OR** have different small groups talk about one and then summarize the discussion for the other groups. **Be sure to have everyone complete View U.**

THE FEAR OF GOD

If you've ever seen *The Wizard of Oz*, you can imagine what the Israelites experienced when God appeared on Mt. Sinai. When Dorothy and her companions meet The Wizard, he frightens them, using a huge green mask, fire, lights, loud music, and a booming voice. We have an expression for The Wizard's theatrics that dates all the way back to Mt. Sinai: The Wizard puts "the fear of God" into Dorothy and her friends.

The Wizard in the movie, of course, proves to be a fraud. He uses technology and illusion to orchestrate his frightening appearance, while he hides in an electrical booth. When his fakery is exposed and confronted, The Wizard's power disappears, and those who have come to see him—even the Cowardly Lion—are no longer afraid.

Some school bullies are much like The Wizard. They instill fear to control people, but on the inside they have nothing to back up their frightening attitude and appearance. Sometimes we fear people such as the school bully more than we fear God.

- What are the roots of fear? What makes people fearful?
- List some of your fears. What, do you think, has caused your fears? How has your faith in God helped you overcome them?
- What is the relationship between fear and control? between fear and faith? between fear and God?
- Does God instill fear in us so that we will believe? Why, or why not? If so, how?
- How appropriate is the word *fear* to describe a relationship with God? Should we never fear God?

JUST TEN? OR ONLY TWO?

The Ten Commandments were only the tip of the iceberg. In Scripture, God actually gives Moses 613 laws for the Israelites to obey. That's a lot of commandments. Many of these rules involved things such as which foods were acceptable to eat and how to make the body ritually clean. Breaking any of these laws carried consequences. No wonder the Pharisees and other religious leaders of Jesus' day seemed so hung up about following the Law so closely.

In Jesus' teaching about the Law, he sums the entire list into two commandments. Read **Mark 12:28-34** and list them below:

1.

2.

- How does keeping the two laws Jesus mentioned "cover you" on all of the other commandments?

Read **Matthew 5:17-48.** Jesus is sometimes referred to as "Matthew's Moses" because he reiterates the Ten Commandments with some new twists.

- How does Jesus make Moses' laws even harder to obey?
- *Why* would Jesus make these laws harder to obey?

62

VIEW C: EVERYONE NEEDS TO KNOW THE RULES

You have probably heard the saying, "Ignorance of the law is no excuse." However, many people are caught in the criminal justice system because they did not know the law. No one taught these people the rules—or perhaps even right from wrong.

Meanwhile, other people succeed (and avoid the criminal justice system) because they understand the rules very well and sometimes know loopholes—how to do what the rules were intended to stop without actually "breaking" the law.

- If people are going to find loopholes in rules, why have rules at all?
- Do you think that ignorance of the law should be an excuse for violating the rules? Why, or why not?
- What rules that you must follow do you like least? Which do you believe are most beneficial? Should you be bound by a rule if you see no benefit in it?
- Why, do you think, was the Law necessary for the ancient Israelites? Why are rules necessary for our society today? Do the same reasons for having laws apply today as applied when Moses received God's commandments?
- How might laws contribute to corruption? How might laws be important in a society?
- Why, do you think, would Paul claim that faithfully obeying the entire Law still wasn't adequate for salvation—and that Jesus gave us something we couldn't obtain by obeying Moses' Law?

LISTEN UP!

Moses acted as liaison between God and the Israelites. Now Jesus serves as the mediator between us and God. Through the "thunder," Christ hears and understands God's voice.

Through Jesus, we talk to God; and through the Holy Spirit, we hear from God. Sometimes God speaks to us through our hearts, our parents, our teachers, our pastors, and our friends; and it sounds like thunder—harsh, loud, confusing, and frightening. We cannot understand everything that God is trying to say to us. Even when God's voice comes to us in a quiet whisper, a prayer, or a hymn, we still have trouble understanding.

Write your reflections on these questions:

- Are you waiting to hear from God? What are you doing to better hear God's voice?

- When has God spoken to you?

- How do you know when you hear God's voice?

- How do you know or understand what God is trying to say?

Listen for God today.

Check www.ileadyouth.com/3V for worship suggestions.

64

GIVE ME A BREAK

Exodus 31:12-17

We live in a fax, e-mail, and cell phone society. We're always busy doing something—soccer, football, cheerleading, basketball, swimming, studying, vacationing, whatever. We've been taught that idle time is unproductive, wasted time. Sometimes we get so overwhelmed that we want to cry out, "Give me a break!" So it should be reassuring to know that even God needed a day to rest and reflect.

¹² The Lord said to Moses, ¹³ You yourself are to speak to the Israelites: "You shall keep my sabbaths, for this is a sign between me and you throughout your generations, given in order that you may know that I, the Lord, sanctify you. ¹⁴ You shall keep the sabbath, because it is holy to you; everyone who profanes it shall be put to death; whoever does any work on it shall be cut off from among the people. ¹⁵ Six days shall work be done, but the seventh day is a sabbath of solemn rest, holy to the Lord; whoever does any work on the sabbath day shall be put to death. ¹⁶ Therefore the Israelites shall keep the sabbath, observing the sabbath throughout their generations, as a perpetual covenant. ¹⁷ It is a sign forever between me and the people of Israel that in six days the Lord made heaven and earth, and on the seventh day he rested, and was refreshed."

Exodus 31:12-17, NRSV

Read the passage aloud. What is your initial reaction to the text?

- What questions does the text raise for you?
- Highlight words or phrases that you feel are important or create questions for you.
- In what tone did God hand out this rule on the sabbath?
- What do you think is the difference between a day of rest and a day of "solemn rest"?

From your reading of this text, imagine what God would do on the sabbath. Make a list of what you think might be God's activities for the day. Be creative and include possible activities from the present day if you wish. As a group, share your lists with one another.

- What new insights into the text did you gain?
- How did the lists of God's imagined activities compare with your usual activities on the sabbath?

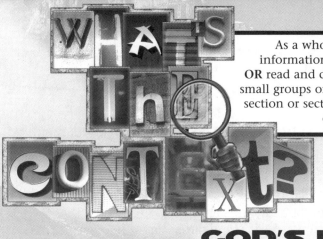

As a whole group, read through this information and discuss the questions; **OR** read and discuss the commentaries in small groups or pairs assigned to a specific section or sections. Then summarize your conversation for the others.

FOLLOW GOD'S EXAMPLE

The Hebrew word *shabbat* means "ceasing, coming to an end of activity or resting." The Greek equivalents are *sabbaton* and *katapausis*, which both mean "rest."

Notice that God has already instituted the sabbath before Moses ever comes to Mt. Sinai. The sabbath begins with Creation, when God rests after making heaven and earth. God is not requiring the people to do something that God does not follow. Rather, God is revealing something of God's nature to the Israelites so they can live holy lives and draw closer to God.

Read **Genesis 2:1-3.**

- Why would a God with infinite power take a rest?
- How do you define rest? Can you participate in work and still rest?
- Why would a day of rest be holy?

SABBATHS AND JUBILEES

Did you notice that God, in speaking to Moses, refers to the sabbath in the plural? What's up with that?

Actually, God establishes three types of sabbaths with the Israelites:

- ❏ the weekly sabbath on the seventh day (**Exodus 20:8; 31:12; 35:1;** and **16:22**);
- ❏ three yearly days of sabbath (**Leviticus 23:23-25** and **23:39**), which could fall on any day of the week;
- ❏ a sabbath every seventh year (**Leviticus 25:1-7**).

In addition to the sabbaths, God ordains that every fiftieth year is to be a year of jubilee (**Leviticus 25:8-16**).

Divide into four groups. Assign to each group one of the types of sabbath or the jubilee year. Each group should read the Scriptures associated with that sabbath listed above and present to the class when that sabbath or jubilee is to be observed and what special instructions God gives about it.

- What new insights did you gain about the sabbath?
- How do all the types of sabbaths relate to the number 7?
- Why does violation of the sabbath carry such harsh penalties?
- How does the jubilee year relate to God's purpose in creating the sabbath?
- How do all of these observances reflect God's order for and authority over Creation?

WHAT DOES IT MEAN TO BE SANCTIFIED AND HOLY?

In establishing the sabbath, God says that not only the day but the people are sanctified. To sanctify something is to set it apart through cleansing or making it holy.

God sets apart the sabbath day not only so that we will remember and reflect upon who *God* is but also so that we will remember who *we* are and what it means to be made holy by God.

- How could observing the sabbath draw you closer to God?
- How does drawing closer to God bring holiness?
- In what ways has God sanctified people?
- What does this text suggest to you about the relationship God wants with us?
- What does it suggest about our relationships with one another?
- Why can we be sanctified only by God?
- How can going to church, Bible study, and other activities with believers draw us into holy living?
- What does it mean to live a holy life?

SABBATH AND COVENANT RELATIONSHIPS

God instructs Moses that the sabbath will serve as a perpetual covenant. To keep their part of the covenant, the people must take time to rest on the sabbath and pass this tradition to future generations.

A covenant does not necessarily mean an agreement between two equal parties. In this case, the Israelites do not enter into this covenant of their own volition; rather, God gives them responsibility for keeping God's sabbath.

- God's part of the covenant is never expressly stated in this text. What do you think it is?

- Why does God place responsibility for keeping the covenant on those who celebrate the sabbath?
- What responsibility did God give parents in keeping this covenant? What religious traditions or practices have your parents passed on to you?
- In what ways do you make covenants with God? How would you compare such covenants to God's covenants with the Israelites?

WHAT IS WORK?

The commandment to do no work on the sabbath creates one obvious question: How do you define *work*?

Today, Jewish people who strictly follow the Orthodox tradition will not drive their cars on the sabbath. Why? Because God said that the people must do no cooking on the sabbath. Cooking meant lighting a fire. The internal combustion engine of an automobile involves sparks that ignite fuel—in a sense, a fire.

On the other hand, the commandment was not interpreted as so strict that people could not feed and water their animals on the sabbath—as Jesus points out to the religious leaders of his day.

The Scriptures also make several exceptions about allowing priests to perform work on the sabbath. Read **Leviticus 24:8; 1 Chronicles 23:31;** and **2 Chronicles 23:4** to find these exceptions.

- What types of activities would you define as work?
- Could the definitions differ for different people? How?
- When would you make an exception to doing no work on the sabbath?
- Why would breaking this commandment carry the punishment of being "put to death"?

JESUS AND THE SABBATH

The religious leaders of his day frequently criticize Jesus for violating the sabbath—often (though not always) for healing people on the sabbath.

Read **Luke 13:10-17; Matthew 12:1-8;** and **9-12.**

- How do Jesus' actions reflect his teaching that the importance of observing the sabbath was to draw us into closer relationship with God?
- What, do you think, did Jesus mean in saying, "The sabbath was made for humankind, and not humankind for the sabbath" (**Mark 2:27**)?
- What did he mean in saying that he was Lord over the sabbath?
- Why, do you think, are the Pharisees so concerned about Jesus' actions on the sabbath? How does their understanding of the sabbath differ from Jesus' teaching?
- What insights do Jesus' actions give you about your own actions on the sabbath?

AFTER READING THE TEXT AND THE CONTEXT...

> Deal with some or all of these questions before moving to What's Next?

- What new insights do you have?
- What answers did you gain to questions you raised earlier?
- What new questions do you have?
- In what ways do you observe the sabbath?
- Why is the sabbath necessary today?
- Why do Christians participate in the sabbath?
- What one learning will you take from this Scripture and apply to your life?

Choose one or more of Views A, B, and C to discuss; **OR** have different small groups talk about one and then summarize the discussion for the other groups. **Be sure to have everyone complete View U.**

VIEW A: HOW DO I OBSERVE THE SABBATH?

Most Christians observe sabbath on Sunday, while others (following the Jewish tradition) observe it on Saturday, the seventh day of the week. The sabbath begins at dusk on the day before the sabbath and continues until sunset the next evening. Some people observe the sabbath by severely restricting their activities, while others enjoy the sabbath through recreation. Jesus teaches that the important thing is to take the time out to draw close to God; that means rest but also making ourselves available to do good for others.

- Why, do you think, has God required us to take a rest?
- How do you find a balance between too much work and too much rest?
- List some ways you observe the sabbath.
- List some ways you take time for God during the week.
- How do our stress loads prevent us from getting rest? How does rest free you to be one of God's people?

VIEW B: MAY I WORK OR SHOP ON THE SABBATH?

Once, almost all businesses in America were closed on Sunday. Today, those that close for sabbath observance—such as Chick-fil-A restaurants and Hobby Lobby stores—are the exception. These businesses sacrifice millions of dollars in revenue by remaining closed on Sunday. Millions of Americans must work on Sunday. And most of us don't think twice about going to the mall or the grocery store or to any other business on a Sunday. What has happened to God's sabbath? And are we partly to blame for the fact that so few Christians observe it?

- What businesses do you know of that close on Sundays? Do you know people who have to work on Sundays?
- How is closing on the sabbath a statement of faith for businesses?
- Can you still observe sabbath even if you have to work?
- Even if you don't work on Sundays, how may you contribute to "profaning" the sabbath?
- Is it wrong to go shopping or to the movies on Sundays? Why, or why not?
- Do you think that American culture should reflect Christian traditions such as sabbath observance? Explain.
- How does celebrating sabbath free us to be God's people?

VIEW C: GIVE ME A BREAK!

In part, the biblical sabbath was a practical and spiritual labor law that protected workers; it was symbolic of God's protection. In **Exodus 12**, God directs sabbath observance toward the labor of servants and animals, who need rest. In Deuteronomy 5, God connects the sabbath to the deliverance of the Israelites from bondage. They were free to take a rest, just as God rested, because they were no longer Pharaoh's slaves.

The sabbath laid a foundation for many of our labor laws that protect workers from being exploited. For example, employers must provide their employees with breaks and lunch periods. Other laws protect children from labor exploitation.

Especially in developing countries, unfortunately, exploitation of child labor is a serious problem. These children work for a variety of reasons, but most often because their families are poor. Although the children are not well paid, they are major contributors to the family household. They work long hours under conditions that are mentally and physically abusive.

- How can someone get paid for working and still be a slave?
- Drawing on the story of the Israelites, what issues related to slavery could apply to a work environment? What makes the child labor situation especially exploitative? How does the sabbath relate to these children?
- Does our desire to pay lower prices for goods contribute to exploitation of laborers? Why, or why not?
- What is the church's role in addressing these issues? What can you do?

CATCHING UP

We get so busy with our daily lives, that Sunday may become our "catch-up day," when we take care of things we didn't get around to during the week. Our calendars are so full that God may become just another appointment we schedule for an hour or two on Sunday. How does that fulfill God's purpose for observing the sabbath?

This week, resolve to find additional time for God. See what you can eliminate in your schedule to make more room for God in your life.

Write your reflections about the following question:

- In what ways areas of my life do I need a closer relationship with God?

Check www.ileadyouth.com/3V for worship suggestions.

A STIFF-NECKED PEOPLE

Exodus 32:7-14

We want to do the right thing. Our intentions are good. Really! When our parents leave us in charge and tell us what they expect us to do (and not do) while they're gone, we don't intend to follow every single instruction. What self-respecting teenager would? But neither do we intend for things to get out of hand. Maybe we'll invite a few friends over, get up a party. It won't hurt to bend the rules a little, will it?

7 The LORD said to Moses, "Go down at once! Your people whom you brought up out of the land of Egypt, have acted perversely;. *8* they have been quick to turn aside from the way that I commanded them; they have cast for themselves an image of a calf, and worshiped it and sacrificed to it, and said, "These are your gods, O Israel, who brought you up out of the land of Egypt!" *9* The LORD said to Moses, "I have seen this people, how stiff-necked they are. *10* Now let me alone, so that my wrath may burn hot against them and I may consume them; and of you I will make a great nation."

11 But Moses implored the LORD his God, and said, "O LORD, why does your wrath burn hot against your people, whom you brought out of the land of Egypt with great power and with a mighty hand? *12* Why should the Egyptians say, 'It was with evil intent that he brought them out to kill them in the mountains, and to consume them from the face of the earth'? Turn from your fierce wrath; change your mind and do not bring disaster on your people. *13* Remember Abraham, Isaac, and Israel, your servants, how you swore to them by your own self, saying to them, 'I will multiply your descendants like the stars of heaven, and all this land that I have promised I will give to your descendants, and they shall inherit it forever.'" *14* And the LORD changed his mind about the disaster that he planned to bring on his people.

Exodus 32:7-14, NRSV

Read the passage aloud.

- What are your initial reactions to this story?
- What questions does the text raise for you?

Review Moses' conversation with God. Retell the conversation in your own words.

- In what kinds of relationships do these types of conversations usually happen?
- What do you think Moses was feeling? What was God thinking?

Invite volunteers to dramatize this story, using a set of different set of facts, involving family or school.

- What stands out in seeing the story from a different perspective?
- How did your understanding of the story change?
- What new insights do you have?

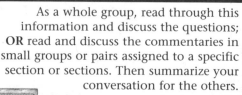

> As a whole group, read through this information and discuss the questions; **OR** read and discuss the commentaries in small groups or pairs assigned to a specific section or sections. Then summarize your conversation for the others.

WHO WAS AARON?

In Hebrew, Aaron's name means "uncertain." Aaron, Moses' brother, was the son of Jochebed and Amram of the tribe of Levi. Although Moses is separated from his family soon after birth, in his later years he manages to reunite with Aaron and their sister Miriam.

Moses, who suffers from a speech impediment, needs Aaron. But Aaron serves as more than Moses' spokesperson. He throws down the staff, which turns into a snake. He initiates several of the Ten plagues. God officially establishes Aaron and his family as Israel's priests.

Aaron and his sons serve as Moses' assistants. The only recorded conflict between Moses and Aaron is the incident centering around the making of the golden calf.

At the age of 123, Aaron dies; and his son Eleazar becomes the priest. The author of Hebrews contrasts the imperfect Aaron with the perfect priesthood of Jesus (**Hebrews 5:7, 11**).

- In what ways do Moses and Aaron complement each other?
- Why would God choose someone who made an idol for the people to be the priestly leader? What does this choice reveal about us and about God?
- How well would you work as an assistant and spokesperson to your brother or sister? Why?
- When have you seen other sibling teams work effectively together? What seemed to make their relationship work?

WHILE THE CAT'S AWAY...

Have you ever had substitute teacher at school? Have you ever taken advantage of one? told him or her about "rules" that didn't exist? played tricks on the sub? made his or her life miserable?

Aaron is the Israelites' "substitute teacher" while Moses is on the mountain. But there's one big difference between Moses and the usual subs: Aaron, who was supposed to be a leader for the people, had "let them run wild" (**Exodus 32:25**). Even as Moses was receiving the commandment from God not to make images for worship, Aaron was producing a golden calf by popular demand.

Worse still, when Moses returns and confronts his brother, Aaron offers excuses. Think of the lamest excuse you have ever offered to a parent or teacher. Now read **Exodus 32:19-24** and put your excuse up against Aaron's.

- What does Aaron say? If you had been Moses, what would you have said in reply?
- Why, do you think, did the Israelites want to make a golden calf?
- How did Moses' long absence give them an excuse?
- Why, do you think, did Aaron go along with it when he should have known better?
- When have you allowed others to sway you into doing something you knew was wrong? What were the consequences?
- Why, do you think, do leaders so often give people what they want, instead of what they need?
- How do our own leaders sometimes act as Aaron did?

82

WHY A BULL?

Why did the Aaron make an idol of a calf? Cows are neither tough nor particularly smart. Why didn't he make a fierce predator like a lion or a soaring figure like an eagle?

In the ancient Near East, many cultures used a young bull to depict a god of fertility. Such goals were believed to ensure that rain would fall, crops would grow and offspring (both among livestock and humans) would be born. Bulls also symbolized strength and dominance within a herd.

Aaron's act was not the last time a leader of Israel would make a golden calf. When the nation split into the Northern Kingdom of Israel and the Southern Kingdom of Judah after Solomon's death, King Jeroboam I of Israel made two calves of gold, built shrines for them and had the people worship there, instead of in the Temple in Jerusalem. Read **1 Kings 12:25-30** for an account of this heresy.

- What "idols" do people worship today, perhaps without realizing it?
- Compare fan attitudes toward teen idols with the worship of an idol by the Israelites. How are they different? How are they similar?
- How can devotion to a symbol, person, or organization get in the way of worshiping God?

DOES GOD NEED ANGER MANAGEMENT?

While Moses is on Mount Sinai receiving God's Law for the Israelites, God sees everything the people are doing below. In fact, Moses finds out from God about the golden calf. God is angry and wants to be alone. Alternately, God wants to destroy the Israelites and make a new covenant with Moses.

- Why would God consider ending the covenant?
- What does this episode reveal about God? about God's people?
- Based on your understanding of God, what seems out of character for God in this story? What seems in character?

Read **Exodus 20:2-6.**

- Why do you think God places these commandments first?
- How does freedom depend on absolute trust in God? How did the Israelites violate that trust?
- In God's eyes, what's so wrong with humans attempting to worship a likeness of God they have made?

Read **Psalm 30:5; 103:8; 145:8; Joel 2:13; and Nahum 1:3.**

- How do these verses add to your understanding of God and God's reaction to the Israelites?

MOSES GOES EGO-TRIPPIN' WITH GOD

Nikki Giovanni, an acclaimed African-American poet, wrote a poem entitled, "Ego-Trippin'." One verse of the poem says, "Even my errors are correct."

That's sort of how we view God. God is all-knowing and all-powerful. God's commands are not even to be questioned.

So it's surprising—even funny—to see Moses not only question God's decision to destroy the Israelites but to use psychology on God. It's as if Moses knows what God cares about and uses that knowledge to change God's mind. God's mind changes! What's up with that?

Read **Exodus 32:11-14**.

Write your own modern-day dialogue between God and Moses. Be creative.

- How does Moses "ego-trip" with God by appealing to God's self-image?
- Why should God care what the Egyptians think?
- How does this conversation affect your image of God? of Moses?
- In the original Hebrew, the words that "God changed his mind" read literally as "The LORD repented of the evil." How does this affect your understanding of the text?

This story isn't the only one in which God's mind changes. Read **Genesis 18:20-33; 2 Kings 20:1-7; and Jonah 3:10** for other examples.

- If God knows and plans everything, how could God's mind change?
- What do these Scriptures suggest about our own relationship with God?

THE CONSEQUENCES OF SIN

Read **Exodus 12:33-36**. Remember the gold and silver the Israelites took when they left Egypt? God grants it to the children of Israel as a blessing. In the study text, we see what they did with it. It must have been especially disappointing to God to see this gift squandered in a way that indicated the people were not yet ready to trust in a God they couldn't see.

Moses burns the golden calf, crushes the ashes into a powder, mixes the powder with water, and makes the Israelites drink it—"a trial by ordeal." Anyone who got sick from drinking the mixture was judged to be guilty.

- Is it significant to you that God does not tell Moses to perform this action and that Moses apparently does it on his own? Explain.

Read **Exodus 32:25-29, 33-35.**

- What other punishments do the Israelites receive?
- In what ways, do you think, does sin bring its own consequences?

86

AFTER READING THE TEXT AND THE CONTEXT . . .

> Deal with some or all of these questions
> before moving to What's Next?

- What new insights do you have?

- What answers did you find to questions you raised earlier?

- What do you admire about Moses in this story?

- How would you define the term *stiff-necked*?

- In threatening to destroy the Israelites, how was God's reputation on the line?

- What does this text suggest about grace? mercy? obedience? leadership?

- How does Moses balance loyalties to God and to the people?

- What one learning will you take from this Scripture and apply to your life?

Choose one or more of Views A, B, and C to discuss; **OR** have different small groups talk about one and then summarize the discussion for the other groups. **Be sure to have everyone complete View U.**

VIEW A — STIFF-NECKED

If you have ever had a stiff neck, you know that it can be a painful experience. And if you've ever known someone who was a pain in the neck, you know that it is also a miserable experience.

The Israelites are rapidly becoming a pain in the neck to both God and Moses.

A stiff neck can affect your body's coordination and limit your ability to move freely. It can also can also make it difficult for you to bow your head. The Israelites who worshiped the golden calf were stiff in the neck spiritually. They were stubborn. They would not give their trust or their loyalty wholly to God. People with stiff-necked mentalities cannot act on faith but only within the rigid confines of their own understanding.

- Write a sentence explaining why you think God referred to the people as "stiff-necked." What does this term mean to you? Compare your answers. What new insights does this definition give you into the text?
- Based on what you know of their experiences since leaving Egypt, what other adjectives would you use to describe the Israelites?
- Where in our society do you see stiff-necked behavior toward God? toward other people?
- When have you been stiff-necked with God? How did that limit you in being free to be God's person?

87

VIEW B: ONE-SIDED RELATIONSHIPS

Have you ever been part of a one-sided relationship? It's frustrating. You seem to do all of the giving, and the other person never contributes anything in return. At first, perhaps, it doesn't bother you. Gradually, however, such relationships try your patience severely.

God and the Israelites have a one-sided relationship. God delivers the Israelites from Egypt and provides for their needs, asking in return only for trust and loyalty. Instead, the people seem to complain every step of the way. Ultimately, they betray their trust by making an idol to worship. It's no wonder that God, sounding exasperated, raises the idea of terminating the relationship and starting a new one with Moses' descendants.

- Why does God hold onto this one-sided relationship?
- In what sense are all human relationships with God one-sided?
- How might God's purpose be served by allowing someone to continue taking advantage of you as the Israelites take advantage of God?
- How would such a relationship *not* serve God's purpose?

NEEDING TO BELONG

The Israelites in the wilderness are still seeking to form a group identity. In the absence of Moses, who helped them develop such an identity, they take things into their own hands with dangerous actions and terrible consequences.

Gang membership statistics have soared in recent years. Although gangs have long been part of low-income communities, membership is also on the rise in middle- to upper-class communities.

Experts attribute this growth to both a growing level of poverty and the deep yearning of young people to feel that they belong. Many teens feel isolated and unprotected, especially in crime-plagued areas. Joining a gang is a way to feel safer and be part of a community.

Gang membership involves rituals and symbols: wearing common colors, initiations (usually involving a criminal act). High school fraternities and sororities—whose membership also is rising—often engage in their own sometimes dangerous rituals, such as physical hazing. For many people, the gang or club identity can become the most important part of their lives.

- Discuss different organizations and clubs to which you belong. Why did you join? How does membership enhance or limit your life? What role does God have in the activities and clubs in which you participate?
- What are the differences between a gang and a high school sorority/fraternity? What are the similarities? List them. What new insights do these lists give you about the story of the Israelites and the golden calf? Why do people need to worship something? Why is the need for ritual part of our identity?
- In what ways do we allow involvement in organizations (even the church) to come between us and the worship of God?

TRUST ME

Moses has been on the mountain an awfully long time. The people aren't sure why he has been gone so long. Neither, apparently, is Aaron. They don't want to wait any longer. So—just like Adam and Eve, just like Abram and Sarai—they try to take matters into their own hands instead of trusting entirely in God.

Have you ever prayed for something and failed to receive an answer from God right away? Or you received a different answer than you hoped for? Sometimes God does not respond in our timeframe and in the way we wish. Living in the freedom to be God's people means that we don't have to yield to the pressure to take things into our own hands. We put our trust in God.

- What answer are you awaiting from God?
- How have you been tempted to stop waiting and take matters into your own hands?

Pray that God will give you the patience to "wait on the Lord" and the joy that comes from knowing you are in God's care.

Check *www.ileadyouth.com/3V* for worship suggestions.